The Boys of Sheriff Street

Jerome Charyn | Illustrated by Jacques de Loustal

DOVER PUBLICATIONS, INC., Mineola, New York

Bibliographical Note

The Boys of Sheriff Street, first published by Dover Publications, Inc., in 2016,
is a republication of the artwork contained in *Les Freres Adamov,* published
by Casterman in 1991. A new English translation of the original French text
has been provided by Jerome Charyn, who also has written an Introduction.

International Standard Book Number

ISBN-13: 978-0-486-80709-6
ISBN-10: 0-486-80709-6

Manufactured in the United States by RR Donnelley
80709601   2016
www.doverpublications.com

CONTENTS

INTRODUCTION
Jerome Charyn

I first discovered Jacques de Loustal through *Barney et la note bleue* (1987), a graphic novel he did with scenarist Philippe Paringaux about Barney Wilen, the brilliant French saxophonist whose father was an American dentist. *Barney* is one of the most poignant graphic novels I have ever read—it tells of the growing isolation of Barney Wilen and reads like a crime novel without an apparent crime. Loustal's images are almost mosaics that he applies to Wilen's tale piece by piece. We move in slow motion, as if a painter such as Matisse had suddenly decided to do a graphic novel. Loustal has an aesthetic—a painterly touch—that most other graphic artists lack. His own art is not about movement. It is about the solitary images in a dream.

After reading *Barney,* I knew right away that I wanted to work with Loustal. It was my good fortune that we had the same editor, Jean-Paul Mougin, and the same publisher, Casterman. I was able to meet with Loustal and propose my own script, "The Boys of Sheriff Street" (*Les Frères Adamov* in its original French title), a perverse tale about a gang of criminals on Manhattan's Lower East Side in the 1930s. I had no desire to repeat the dynamics of *Barney et la note bleue,* but I didn't want to lose Loustal's wonderful sense of the mosaic. I wanted to tell a crime story in stop-time, a slow motion universe where the gangsters were part of a primitive revenge tale, almost as if they had been ripped out of Greek tragedy.

There's very little dialogue. My gangsters could be part of some forlorn ballet. I didn't want to enter a realistic landscape with Loustal. The Lower East Side almost exists as a stage prop. Much of the action takes place at Mendel's, a café on Sheriff Street, where the patrons are like sleepwalkers suddenly jolted out of their dream state by the appearance of Ida Chance, a cashier at a local movie house. Ida has her own savage beauty, which is apparent to everyone at the café.

All the action revolves around Ida and the chiefs of the Sheriff Street clan, Max and Morris Adamov, a pair of twins. Max was born with a hump on his back; he's the brains of the gang, and the emperor of the Lower East Side. Ida, alas, belongs to his twin brother. But Max can't survive without Ida Chance. And he can only win her by courting destruction.

Ida has a decorative élan in Loustal's designs. He flattens the décor until each of his images is like a tiny poem. The characters in *The Boys of Sheriff Street* are never in control of their destiny. They dance around their own primitive urges—and Loustal has captured these urges in drawings and pastel-like colors that have all the staccato lyricism of jazz. So finally there is a connection between *Barney* and *The Boys of Sheriff Street,* a lyric pull that's almost like musical notes.

Les Frères Adamov was first published in 1991, and it has taken twenty-five years for it to cross the Atlantic. Loustal is an accomplished painter as well as a graphic artist, and he has done many covers and sketches for *The New Yorker,* where his unique style is immediately apparent—buildings that look like vast, empty caverns; animals with their unique reptilian shape; women with a strange, anarchic beauty; men in a permanent dream state. Loustal was an architecture student before he turned to graphic art. He has traveled around the world many times, and is known for his sketchbooks about these voyages. And one might even consider *The Boys of Sheriff Street* as Loustal's private notebook about New York.

The Boys of Sheriff Street

Chapter One
The Arrival of Ida Chance

SHERIFF STREET, 1936. A LONELY LITTLE ISLAND UNDER THE WILLIAMSBURG BRIDGE ON MANHATTAN'S LOWER EAST SIDE. ONE CAN ALMOST IMAGINE IT IN A HALF FORGOTTEN FAIRY TALE. SHERIFF STREET, CUT OFF FROM THE REST OF THE WORLD, HAS ITS OWN CANTEEN: MENDEL'S CAFÉ, A LAIR FOR COCKROACHES, WHORES, ALCOHOLICS, GANGSTERS, AND GUNMEN. NOW, COME INTO THE CAFÉ!

THE HABITUÉS OF MENDEL'S SLOUCH LIKE SLEEPWALKERS WITH AN EMPTY LOOK IN THEIR EYES.

MAX ADAMOV, THE EMPEROR OF MENDEL'S CAFÉ.

SAMSON MCQUEEN, KNOWN AS "QUEENIE,"
THE EMPEROR'S MOST TRUSTED TRIGGERMAN.

WHERE'S MY BROTHER?

AT THE MOVIES, MAX.

AT MENDEL'S QUEENIE HAS CERTAIN PRIVILEGES. HE CAN INTRUDE UPON THE EMPEROR'S PRIVATE TERRITORY.

HE HAS TO BE HERE.

HE WON'T BE LATE, MAX. YOU KNOW MORRIS. HE ALWAYS HAS TO SEE A FILM TWICE.

THERE'S A CERTAIN BEAUTY ABOUT MAX AND HIS HUMPED BACK, A BEAUTY THAT'S VERY ODD. HIS DEFORMITY HAS TURNED HIM INTO A MARVELOUS BIRD OF PREY.

SOMETHING IS GOING TO PLUCK THESE WALKING GHOSTS OF MENDEL'S OUT OF THEIR SLUGGISH HABITS.

MORRIS ADAMOV AND HIS NEW MISTRESS, IDA CHANCE-- A BLONDE WITH A SAVAGE BEAUTY. AN ELECTRIC CURRENT JOLTS THE CAFÉ.

MAX'S TWIN, MORRIS, BORN WITHOUT A BUMP ON HIS BACK.

5

HELLO, MADEMOISELLE.

DROP THE FORMALITIES. SHE'S IDA, IDA CHANCE, THE NEW CASHIER AT THE LOEW'S DELANCEY. THAT'S HOW WE MET. I TAPPED ON THE WINDOW OF HER BOOTH AND INTRODUCED MYSELF.

LITTLE BROTHER, TARTS AREN'T WELCOME HERE, NOT AT MENDEL'S. THEY HAVE TO DRINK IN THE BACK ROOM.

THE EMPEROR BEGINS TO TREMBLE. IDA CHANCE IS ALREADY COURSING THROUGH HIS VEINS AND HAS TURNED HIS BLOOD INTO BLACK INK, BLACK AS THE SKY OVER SHERIFF STREET.

IDA SMILES AND DOESN'T SAY A WORD. SHE ISN'T AFRAID OF EMPERORS. SHE BELONGS TO MORRIS.

YOU'VE MADE A BLUNDER, MAX. YOU'RE TALKING ABOUT MY FIANCÉE.

MORRIS CAN FEEL A FURY ROIL THROUGH HIM.

YOU NEVER SPOKE TO ME OF IDA.

HOW COULD I? WE MET TONIGHT AND DECIDED TO GET ENGAGED.

THE EMPEROR HAS LOST FACE IN HIS OWN CAFÉ. A BLUE VEIN PULSES IN HIS TEMPLE. HE'S BEEN DISGRACED.

WE NOW HAVE A REAL FAMILY. MY GOD, THE LITTLE BROTHER IS ENGAGED! LET'S DRINK TO THEIR HAPPINESS. WHY THE HELL ARE YOU WAITING, YOU GUYS!

QUEENIE TRIES TO CALM MAX. BUT HE'S ALSO FALLEN IN LOVE WITH IDA, LIKE EVERYONE ELSE AT THE CAFÉ.

A HUNDRED YEARS OF HAPPINESS FOR THE LUCKY COUPLE!

NO, TWO HUNDRED! TWO HUNDRED YEARS OF HAPPINESS.

DUMMY, NO ONE EVER SURVIVES THAT LONG!

GOD WILL MAKE AN EXCEPTION. GOD LOVES THE ADAMOVS!

TO YOUR HAPPINESS, MORRIS!

NOW ONE CAN SENSE THE FUROR OF MENDEL'S CAFÉ, THE LAUGHTER, THE CLINKING GLASSES OF BEER, THAT FORBIDDEN DESIRE ON EVERYONE'S FACE.

GENTLEMEN, IT'S TIME TO SPEAK ABOUT BUSINESS.

THE WHISKEY DOESN'T WARM UP MAX'S SOUL. THE BLOOD COURSES THROUGH HIS VEINS, STILL AS DARK AS A SIGHTLESS SKY.

JEAN HARLOW AND GEORGE RAFT, THE NEW PRINCES OF HOLLYWOOD.
GLACIAL CREATURES--IMMACULATE, BEAUTIFUL, AND UTTERLY REMOTE.

THE ENTIRE CAFÉ LOOKS AT IDA'S REFLECTION
IN THE MIRROR--GLACIAL AND GORGEOUS AS THE
IMAGES IN THE MAGAZINES. COMPLETELY UNDER
HER SPELL, THEY NOW HAD THEIR OWN MOVIE STAR.
IDA IS THE DUCHESS OF SHERIFF STREET, AS SAVAGE
AND REMOTE AS HER REFLECTION. A BEAUTIFUL
BEAST READY TO POUNCE AND BURST RIGHT
THROUGH THE ROOF. POOR MENDEL'S, POOR MAX.

ASA'S OF ATTORNEY STREET, THE BIGGEST DELICATESSEN ON THE PLANET.

MIDNIGHT.

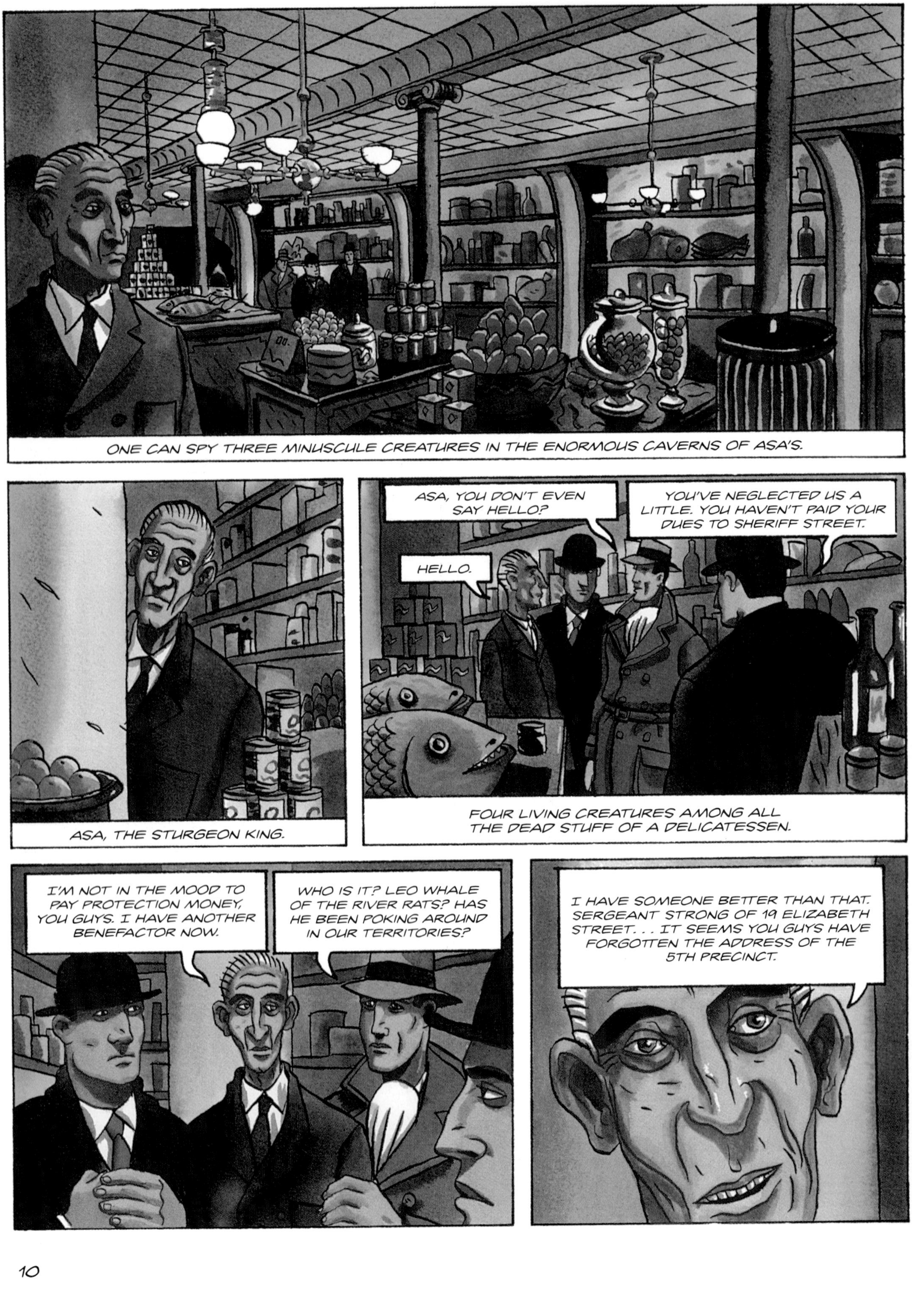
ONE CAN SPY THREE MINUSCULE CREATURES IN THE ENORMOUS CAVERNS OF ASA'S.
ASA, THE STURGEON KING.
ASA, YOU DON'T EVEN SAY HELLO?
YOU'VE NEGLECTED US A LITTLE. YOU HAVEN'T PAID YOUR DUES TO SHERIFF STREET.
HELLO.
FOUR LIVING CREATURES AMONG ALL THE DEAD STUFF OF A DELICATESSEN.
I'M NOT IN THE MOOD TO PAY PROTECTION MONEY, YOU GUYS. I HAVE ANOTHER BENEFACTOR NOW.
WHO IS IT? LEO WHALE OF THE RIVER RATS? HAS HE BEEN POKING AROUND IN OUR TERRITORIES?
I HAVE SOMEONE BETTER THAN THAT. SERGEANT STRONG OF 19 ELIZABETH STREET. . . IT SEEMS YOU GUYS HAVE FORGOTTEN THE ADDRESS OF THE 5TH PRECINCT.

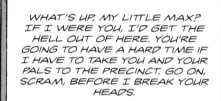

WHAT'S UP, MY LITTLE MAX? IF I WERE YOU, I'D GET THE HELL OUT OF HERE. YOU'RE GOING TO HAVE A HARD TIME IF I HAVE TO TAKE YOU AND YOUR PALS TO THE PRECINCT. GO ON, SCRAM, BEFORE I BREAK YOUR HEADS.

IT'S NOT VERY NICE TO THREATEN US, SERGEANT. WE'RE A PEACE-LOVING GANG. SINCE WHEN ARE YOU PROVIDING PROTECTION FOR FISHMONGERS?

SINCE NOW.

MAX HAS THE BAREST OUTLINE OF A SMILE. THE EMPEROR IS IMPASSIVE, UNTOUCHABLE, AND TERRIFYING.

11

MAX AND ASA WATCH THE BATTLE, LIKE A PAIR OF UMPIRES.

THAT'S ENOUGH! FOR CHRIST'S SAKE, CUT IT OUT!

ALL THE WIVES OF SHERIFF STREET ARE THERE, LIKE LANTERNS IN THE DARK.

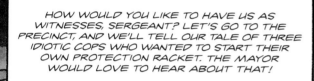

HOW WOULD YOU LIKE TO HAVE US AS WITNESSES, SERGEANT? LET'S GO TO THE PRECINCT, AND WE'LL TELL OUR TALE OF THREE IDIOTIC COPS WHO WANTED TO START THEIR OWN PROTECTION RACKET. THE MAYOR WOULD LOVE TO HEAR ABOUT THAT!

WE'LL TALK AGAIN, MAX.

AND NOW WE HAVE TO RECONSIDER YOUR CONTRIBUTION. THE SIDEWALKS OF SHERIFF STREET ARE IN TERRIBLE SHAPE. WE HAVE TO REPAIR THEM.

THE SKELETON PAYS IN CASH.

COME ON IN, MY PRETTY ONES, AND HELP YOURSELVES. STURGEON, LOX, IT'S ON ME. TELL ASA TO PUT IT ON MY TAB.

YET ANOTHER VICTORY FOR THE BOYS OF SHERIFF STREET.

MORRIS, SHE WASN'T SUPPOSED TO BE AT MY PARTY. WHO INVITED HER?

I DID. SHE'LL BE A BRIDE ONE DAY. AND SHE'LL BELONG WITH THE OTHER WIVES OF SHERIFF STREET.

HIGH NOON ON DELANCEY STREET. WE CAN HEAR THE LIVING HEART OF THE LOWER EAST SIDE.

YOU CAN TALK TO IDA LATER. WE'RE HERE TO SEE THE FILM.

THE BOYS WALK RIGHT AROUND THE CASHIER'S BOOTH. THEY HAVE A LIFETIME PASS AT THE DELANCEY.

15

A COLOSSAL CATHEDRAL DECORATED WITH CHANDELIERS, SURROUNDED BY CANDY BOOTHS.

THE LOEW'S DELANCEY, AN ENORMOUS CAVERN DIVIDED INTO LITTLE CAVES.

WILD BILL HICKOK IN THE ROLE OF GARY COOPER.

THERE'S A RIP IN THE SCREEN. WILD BILL HAS VANISHED.

Refund! REFUND!

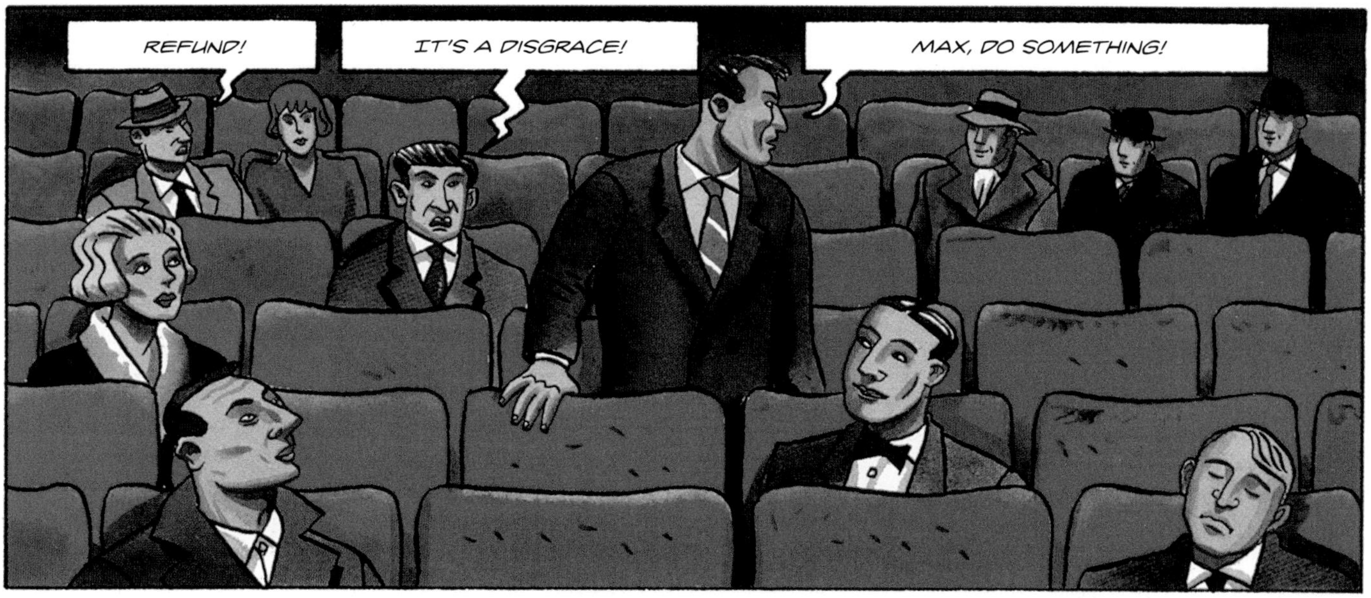
REFUND!
IT'S A DISGRACE!
MAX, DO SOMETHING!

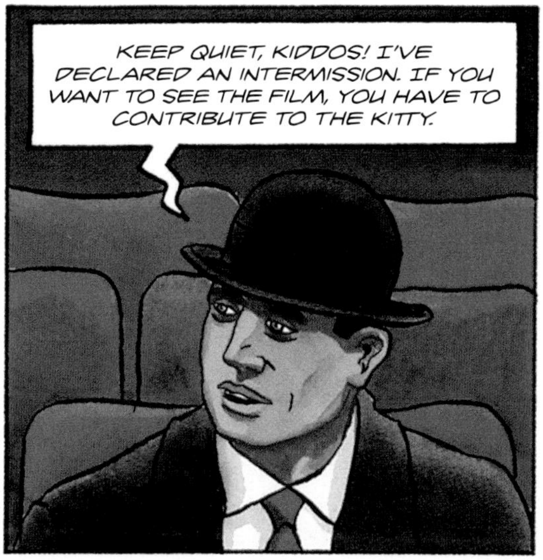
KEEP QUIET, KIDDOS! I'VE DECLARED AN INTERMISSION. IF YOU WANT TO SEE THE FILM, YOU HAVE TO CONTRIBUTE TO THE KITTY.

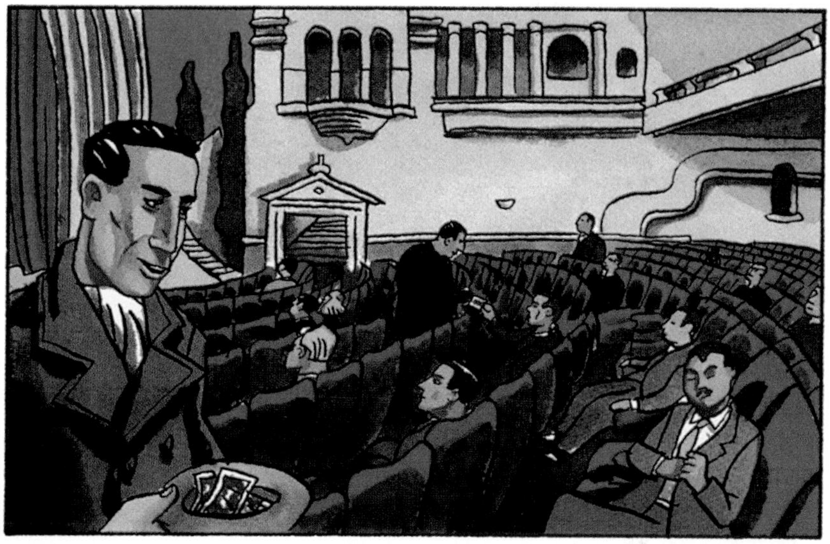

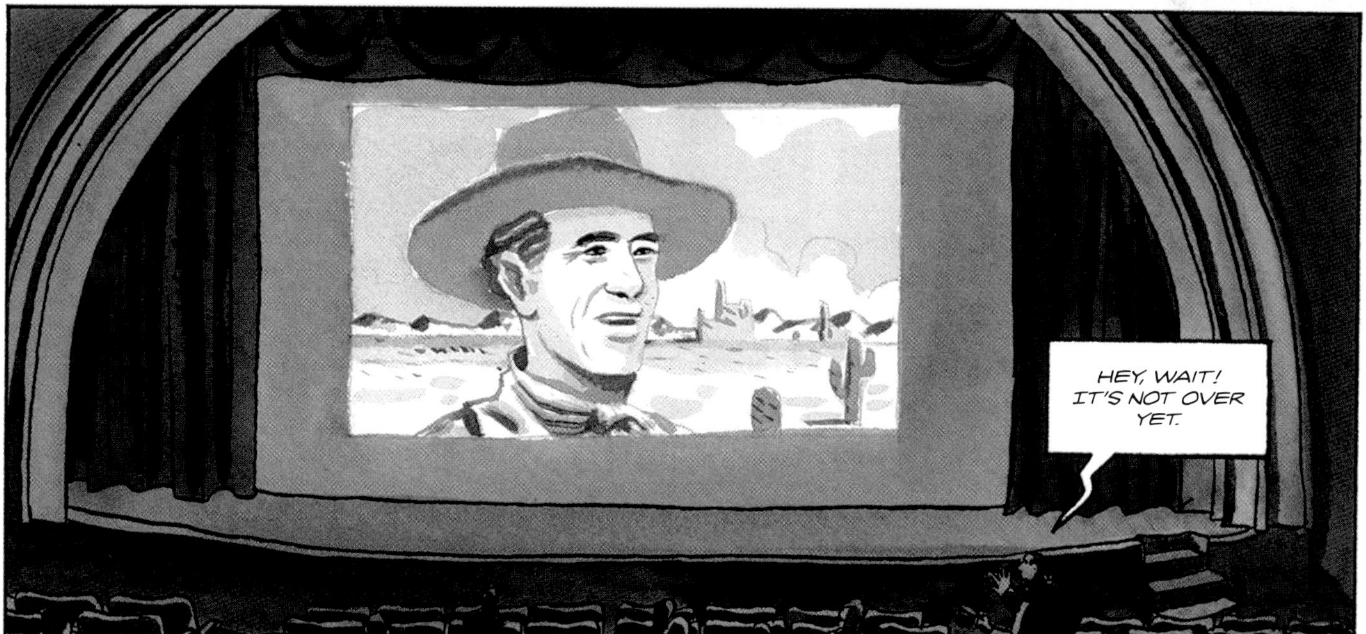
HEY, WAIT! IT'S NOT OVER YET.

IDA CHANCE HAS UTTERLY DESTROYED THE EMPEROR'S APPETITE TO BE ALIVE.

IDA, READY TO DEVOUR THE WORLD.

IDA, I HAVE SOMETHING FOR YOU.

I CALL HIM SWIFTY. HE'S MY FRIEND.

TAKE IT, IDA. SWIFTY'S FOR YOU.

I DON'T LIKE LITTLE ANIMALS, MAX, PARTICULARLY METAL ONES.

MAX HAS ONE OF HIS FAINTING FITS, THE FIRST IN TWO YEARS.

PLEASE, IDA. MAXIE BOUGHT THE LITTLE GUY FOR YOU.

IDA'S HAND SNAPS UP THE TOY MOUSE LIKE THE JAWS OF A SAVAGE BEAST.

MAX, YOU'VE WORKED YOURSELF TO THE BONE. YOU THINK TOO MUCH. YOU'LL MAKE YOURSELF SICK. WHEN A GUY HAS A BRAIN LIKE YOURS, IT HAS TO BE RESTED. WE SHOULD GO ON A VACATION--TO MIAMI BEACH.

WITH HER?

YOU WOULDN'T WANT ME TO LEAVE MY FIANCÉE ALL ALONE, WOULD YOU, MAXIE?

THE SEA KISSED THE SKY AT SOME POINT OF INFINITY THAT NO ONE COULD REACH,
NOT EVEN WITH AN EMPEROR'S VAST DESIRE.

MAX IS AS ALONE IN MIAMI AS HE WAS ON SHERIFF STREET.
IDA IS NEAR HIM AND HE DOESN'T HAVE A MOMENT OF PEACE.

THE EMPEROR DECIDES TO DROWN HIMSELF.

WHO WILL SAVE HIM? MORRIS CAN'T SWIM.

MAX'S AFFLICTION ARISES OUT OF THE WATER.
AN INFERNAL BUMP OF SKIN.

MAXIE, YOU SCARED US TO DEATH. PROMISE YOU'LL NEVER DO THAT AGAIN.

I PROMISE.

Chapter Two
The War With Leo Whale

PENNSYLVANIA STATION, NEW YORK. MAX, MORRIS, AND IDA RETURN FROM MIAMI. UNDER THE METAL SKY OF THE STATION, THE EMPEROR REDISCOVERS HIS BELOVED KINGDOM OF SHADOWS.

MENDEL'S IS REBORN. THE EMPEROR HAS RETURNED WITH HIS RETINUE, AND THE SLEEPWALKERS ROUSE THEMSELVES. EVERYONE'S GAZE IS ON IDA.

ONCE AGAIN, THE CAFÉ FALLS UNDER HER SPELL.

HEY, KIDDOS, WE HAVE TO TALK.

THE EMPEROR'S OFFICE. ONLY A RAT, OR A PRINCE OF SHADOWS, WOULD CHOOSE TO LIVE HERE.

THE WELL IS DRY.

WHAT ARE YOU TRYING TO SAY, MAXIE?

THE WELL IS DRY.

MORRIS, FOR CHRIST'S SAKE, PLEASE ASK YOUR BROTHER TO EXPLAIN? YOU'D HAVE TO KNOW THE BIBLE BY HEART TO FIGURE OUT HIS PUZZLES. THE LORD HIMSELF WOULDN'T BE ABLE TO UNDERSTAND MAX.

DON'T TALK ABOUT GOD IN MY OFFICE.

THEN BE A LITTLE CLEARER, MAX.

OUR VAULTS ARE EMPTY. WE DON'T HAVE A DIME. WE HAVE TO DO SOMETHING ABOUT IT.

OKAY, WHAT DO YOU SUGGEST?

MORRIS AND QUEENIE LOOK LIKE GIANTS NEAR MAX'S MINIATURE DESK.

WE HAVE TO RAID ALL THE SHOPKEEPERS ON GRAND STREET AND CONVINCE THOSE BASTARDS TO CONTRIBUTE A LITTLE MORE TO OUR TREASURY. OUR FUTURE DEPENDS ON THOSE GUYS.

MAX, GRAND STREET IS ON THE BORDERLINE OF LEO WHALE'S TERRITORY. WE'VE BEEN AT PEACE WITH THE RIVER RATS FOR QUITE A WHILE. WE COULD REALLY PISS LEO OFF. WHAT DO YOU THINK, MORRIS?

THE ONE THING I KNOW IS THAT I LIKE LEO WHALE.

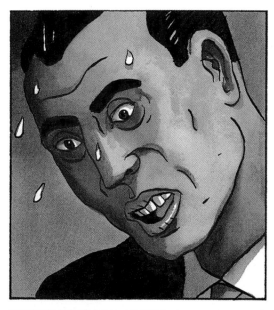

THE EMPEROR SUDDENLY HAS ONE OF HIS SEIZURES.

MAXIE, GET UP.
MAX, PLEASE . . .

QUEENIE,
YOU TELL
HIM
TO GET UP.

IT'S OKAY, MAX.
WE'LL RAID GRAND STREET.

LIKE SOME KIND OF MIRACLE, THE EMPEROR REVIVES HIMSELF.

THAT WILL BE A DOWRY FOR IDA. I CAN'T LET MY BROTHER GET MARRIED WITH PEANUTS IN HIS POCKET. AND THE BOYS WILL HAVE TO MAKE A CONTRIBUTION TO THE NEWLYWEDS.

HEY, WHO THE HELL SPOKE OF MARRIAGE? I *like* AN ENGAGEMENT THAT LASTS A LONG TIME.

WAR HAS BEEN DECLARED. BUT THE BOYS OF SHERIFF STREET DON'T KNOW IF THAT WILL GIVE THEM ENOUGH TIME TO THINK ABOUT IDA.

GRAND STREET, THE DISTRICT OF BRIDAL SHOPS. THE BRIDES IN THE WINDOWS GAZE AT MAX AND HIS GANG. THE EMPEROR IS BLIND TO THESE BRIDES. LIKE A MAGICIAN, HE HOLDS HIS GANG BY HIS OWN INVISIBLE STRING.

THE HELL WITH LEO WHALE, AND THE HELL WITH THE COPS. IF YOU WANT TO STAY IN BUSINESS, YOU'D BETTER GO ALONG WITH ME.

MAX SCREAMS, AND MAX IS VIOLENT, BUT HE'S LIKE A MANNEQUIN, THE FIANCÉ OF ALL THESE ABANDONED BRIDES.

THE EMPEROR'S BALD FIANCÉE.

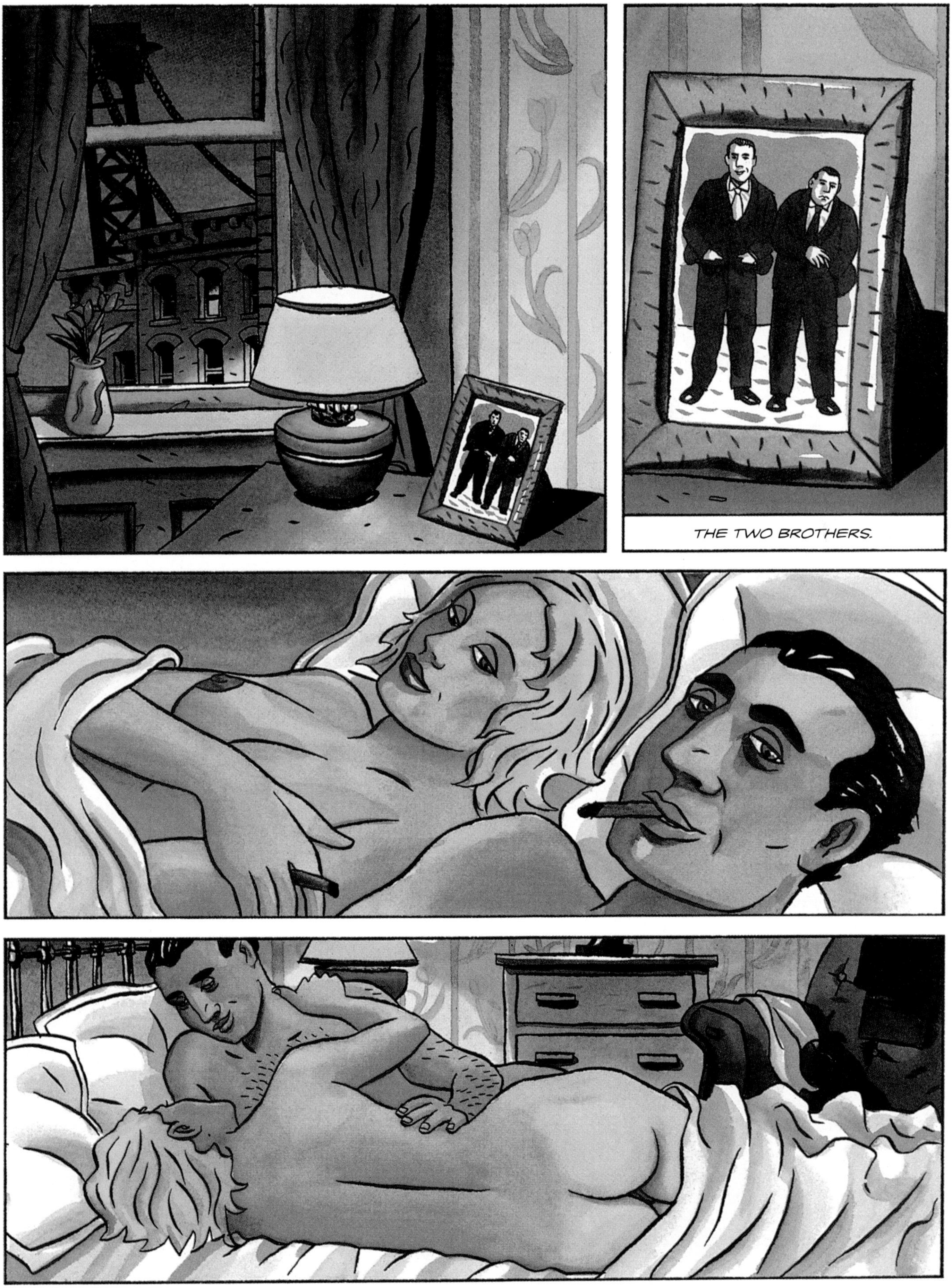
THE TWO BROTHERS.

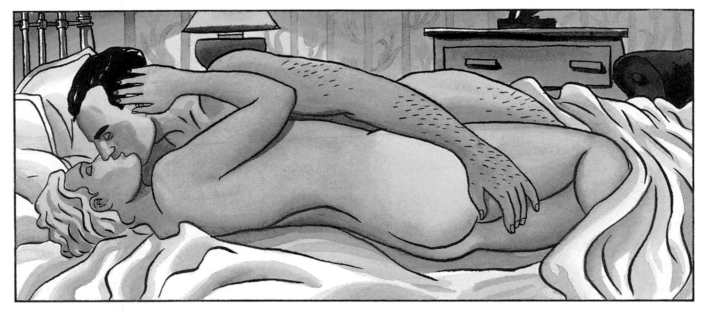

THE HANDSOME GIANT HAS MANAGED TO CAPTURE IDA CHANCE.

THE EMPEROR MAKES HIS ENTRANCE. IT SEEMS AS IF HE'S COMING OUT OF A COMA.

HASN'T ANYBODY EVER TAUGHT YOU HOW TO KNOCK? THIS IS MORRIS'S APARTMENT, YES OR NO?

I NEVER HAD TO KNOCK ON HIS DOOR.

IT'S DIFFERENT NOW.

MORRIS, TELL HIM THAT IT'S DIFFERENT NOW.

DIFFERENT . . .

CAUGHT BETWEEN EMPEROR MAX AND IDA CHANCE, THE WOMAN HE'S CRAZY ABOUT, MORRIS CAN'T MAKE UP HIS MIND.

A PRESENT.

THE BRIDE'S WEDDING DRESS. I PICKED IT MYSELF.

IDA, TELL HIM THAT YOU LOVE THE DRESS.

TELL HIM THAT YOU LOVE IT.

I LIKE IT. BUT TELL YOUR BROTHER TO GET THE FUCK OUT OF HERE.

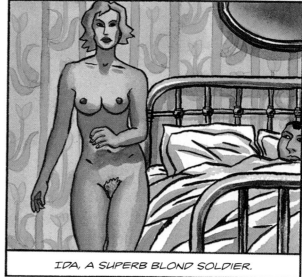

IDA, A SUPERB BLOND SOLDIER.

I HATE IT,
I **hate** IT!

POOR MANNEQUIN, POOR MAX.

THE EMPEROR CROSSES HIS DOMAIN. HIS BLOOD HAS BEGUN TO CONGEAL. HE HAS NO MORE
TERRITORY. HE'S BECOME A LOST CHILD IN STREETS THAT ONCE BELONGED TO HIM. IDA HAS
DUG INTO HIS FLESH AND IS DEVOURING HIM LITTLE BY LITTLE. HE CAN'T SURVIVE WITHOUT HER.

QUEENIE, SEND SOMEONE TO FIND MORRIS. RIGHT NOW!

I'M NOT HAPPY.

WHAT'S THE MATTER NOW? HAVEN'T WE SETTLED YOUR ACCOUNTS?

NO!

I'M NOT CRAZY ABOUT OUR PACT WITH THE RIVER RATS. LEO WHALE'S EMPIRE IS TOO BIG, AND MINE IS TOO SMALL.

DAMMIT, YOUR TERRITORY IS DOUBLE THE SIZE OF HIS.

MAYBE, BUT LEO WANDERS INTO MINE WHENEVER HE WANTS. DOUBLE THE SIZE STILL ISN'T ENOUGH. WE HAVE TO SHOW HIM WHO'S THE REAL BOSS.

AND HOW DO WE ACCOMPLISH THAT?

WE ORGANIZE A LITTLE RAID ON WATER STREET.

THE BOYS OF SHERIFF STREET HAVE ENTERED THE DOMAIN OF LEO WHALE,
A NEW CONTINENT FOR THESE EXPLORERS, NOW A WRECKING CREW.

DO YOU RECOGNIZE US?

OF COURSE. YOU'RE THE BOYS OF SHERIFF STREET. WHAT DO YOU WANT, MISTER MAX?

NOTHING. JUST WARN LEO WHALE THAT WE'VE COME BY TO SAY HELLO.

DROWNING IN HIS LITTLE POOL OF BEER, THIS GUY KNOWS IT ISN'T ALWAYS POSSIBLE TO UNDERSTAND WHAT AN EMPEROR SAYS.

LATE AFTERNOON AT MENDEL'S. IDA ISN'T BEHIND HER CASHIER'S BOOTH AT THE LOEW'S DELANCEY. IT'S HER DAY OFF. LIKE SOME JEAN HARLOW TUMBLING DOWN FROM THE MOON, SHE'S COME TO DISPLAY HER GLACIAL BEAUTY AMONG THE SLEEPWALKERS AT MENDEL'S. THE EMPEROR IS ALONE. HIS BODY WRITHES WHEN HE LOOKS AT IDA. HE NO LONGER HAS THE SIMPLEST PLAN IN MIND. HIS GANG MEANS NOTHING TO HIM AND NEITHER DOES HIS OWN MISERABLE DESTINY.

THE EMPEROR IS FRIGHTENED OF HIS REFLECTION. HE'S FORGOTTEN WHATEVER PROMISES HE'S MADE. HE MUST HAVE IDA CHANCE OR DIE.

LEO WHALE OF THE RIVER RATS.

ONE GLANCE AND LEO FALLS IN LOVE WITH IDA.

HELLO, MISS. WHAT'S YOUR NAME?

CUT IT OUT, LEO. SHE BELONGS TO MORRIS.

TOO BAD.

WHAT CAN WE DO FOR YOU?

I'D LIKE TO KNOW WHY YOU'VE GONE NEAR THE WATERFRONT. I'M A PEACEFUL FELLAH. I NEVER LEAVE THE DOCKS. I THOUGHT WE HAD A TRUCE.

WHAT'S HAPPENED TO YOU, LEO? ARE YOU IN SOME KIND OF A FUNK? THERE'S NO MORE TRUCE. YOUR GLORY DAYS ARE OVER. YOU'VE ALWAYS BEEN PATHETIC. YOU HEAR ME? YOU STINK, LEO.

REPEAT THAT, LITTLE MAN.

YOU STINK, LEO.

THE CAFÉ IS PARALYZED, AS IF IT'S BEEN JINXED.

QUEENIE IS LOST IN HIS OWN SOMBER THOUGHTS. HE KNOWS THAT MAX'S BELLIGERENCE MEANS A WAR WITH LEO WHALE. AH, IT'S THE END OF THE LINE.

Chapter Three
The Fiancée of the Emperor

—

A WAVE OF DERBIES ARRIVES ON THE DOCKS:
THE BOYS OF SHERIFF STREET OCCUPY THE TERRITORY OF LEO WHALE.

IT'S THOSE CRAZY GUYS! MAX'S GANG!

QUEENIE HASN'T JOINED THE FRAY. AN ICE-COLD SHIVER TRAVELS THROUGH HIS BODY. HERE ARE THE CONSEQUENCES OF MAX'S MAD QUEST.

THE RIVER RATS, PHANTOMS OF THE DOCKS, RISE UP FROM NOWHERE.

GUYS, THE HOUR OF MAX'S DOWNFALL HAS COME.

LEO WHALE, THE OTHER EMPEROR, WANTS HIS REVENGE.

HERE'S A LITTLE SOMETHING. YOU SHOULDN'T HAVE RIPPED OFF MY CLOTHES.

LEO STRIKES WITH HIS CLUB.
THE SOUND OF THE BLOW REVERBERATES IN THE TWILIGHT LIKE A LONG, MERCILESS GROAN.

THE EMPEROR'S BROTHER IS SERENE AS HE LIES DEAD, ALMOST AS SERENE AS WHEN HE WAS STILL ALIVE.

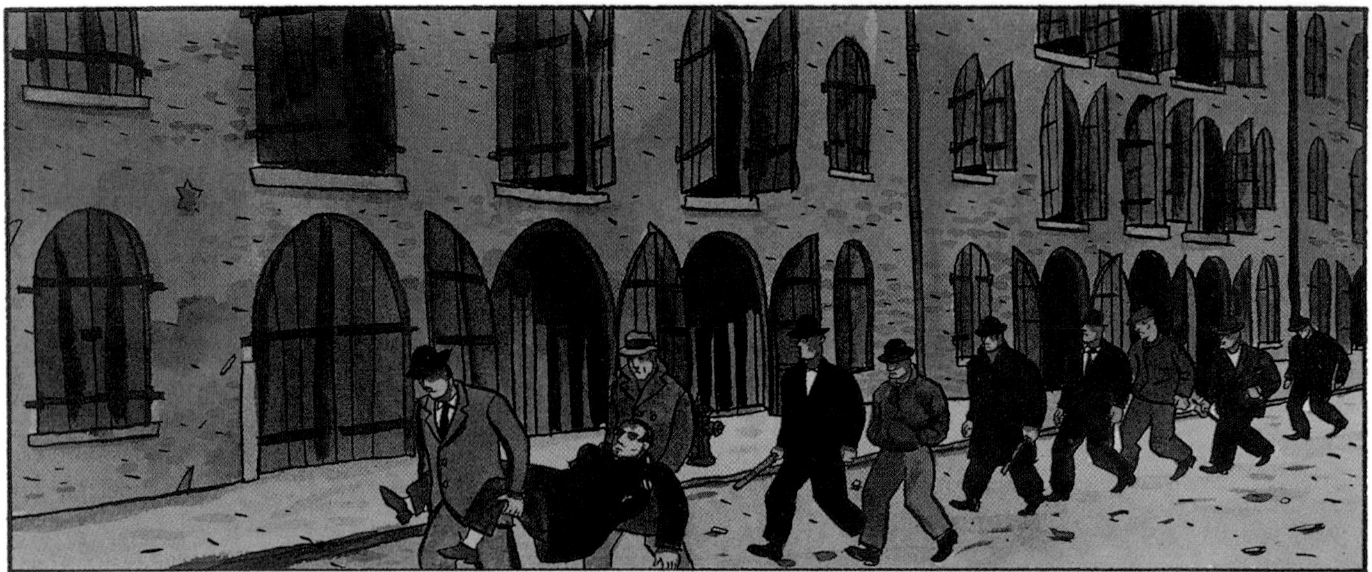

ALREADY THE BOYS OF SHERIFF STREET BEGIN TO MOURN.

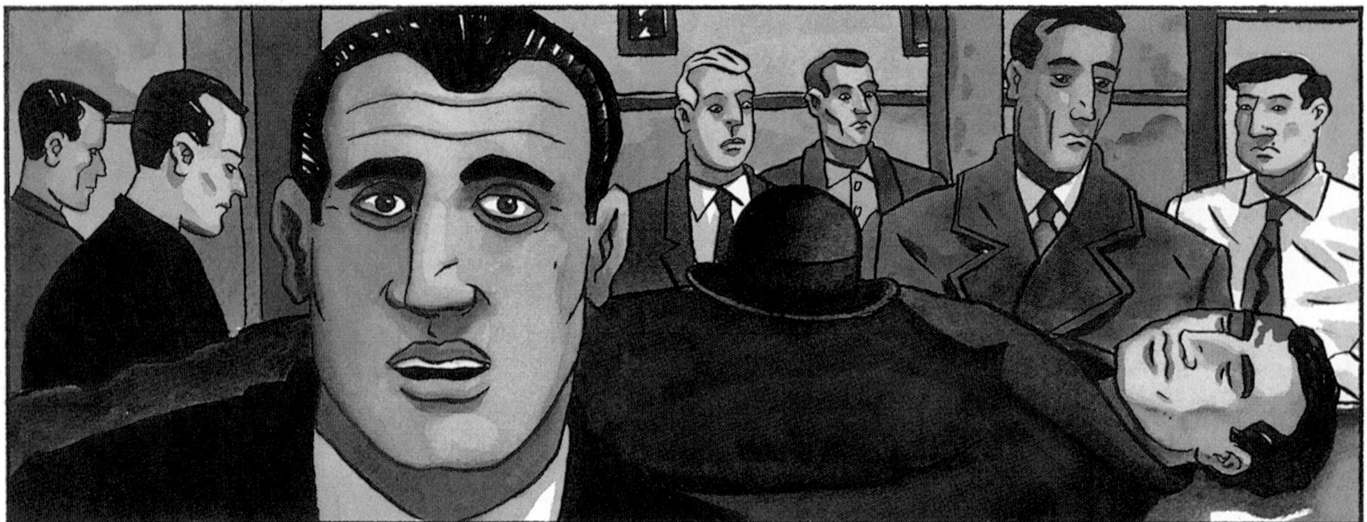

MAX DOESN'T KNOW WHAT DO ABOUT HIS REMORSE. HE LOOKS LIKE MORE OF A GHOST THAN HIS DEAD BROTHER.

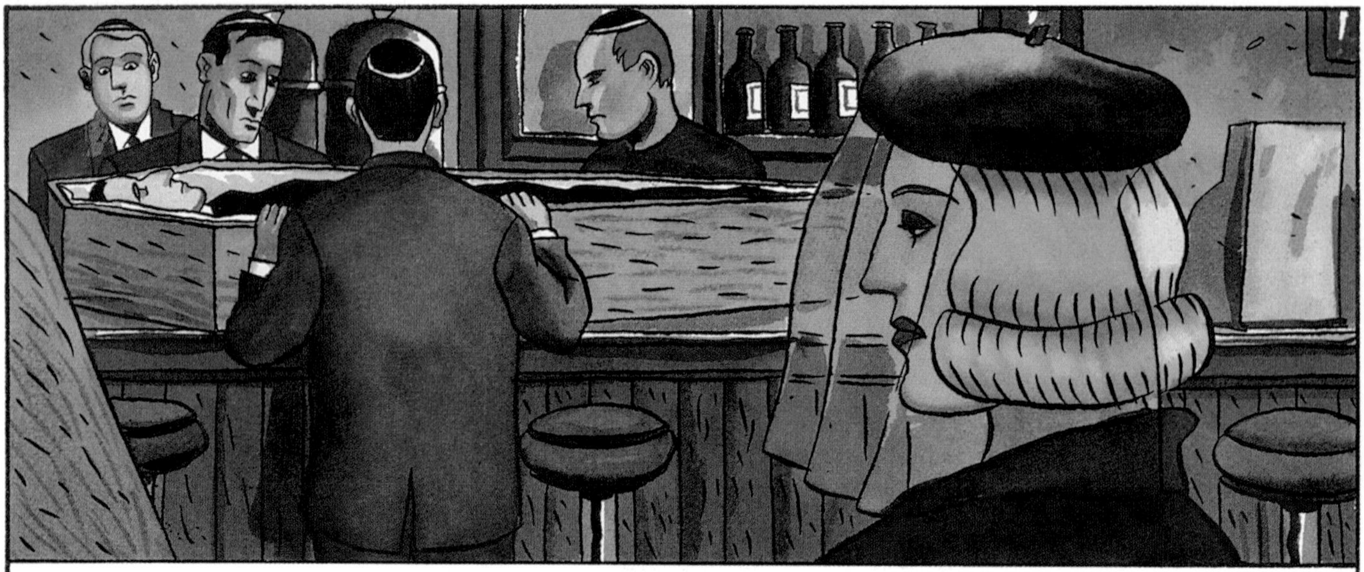

IDA. ALONE.

WE'RE INCONSOLABLE, MISTER MAX. WE LOVED YOUR BROTHER, LOVED HIM A LOT. LEO WHALE OUGHT TO ROT IN HELL.

THE EMPEROR DOESN'T LISTEN. HE IS HIS OWN CAPTIVE. HIS GIGANTIC DOMAIN HAS BEEN REDUCED INTO A LAYER OF REGRET. HE WALKS AND HAS NO IDEA WHERE TO GO.

STAY OUT OF THIS, SAMSON MCQUEEN. I HAVE AN ACCOUNT TO SETTLE.

WHAT KIND OF ACCOUNT?

SOMETHING PRIVATE. I'M PREPARING THE DEATH OF A CERTAIN LEO.

YOU INTEND TO ATTACK LEO ALL BY YOURSELF?

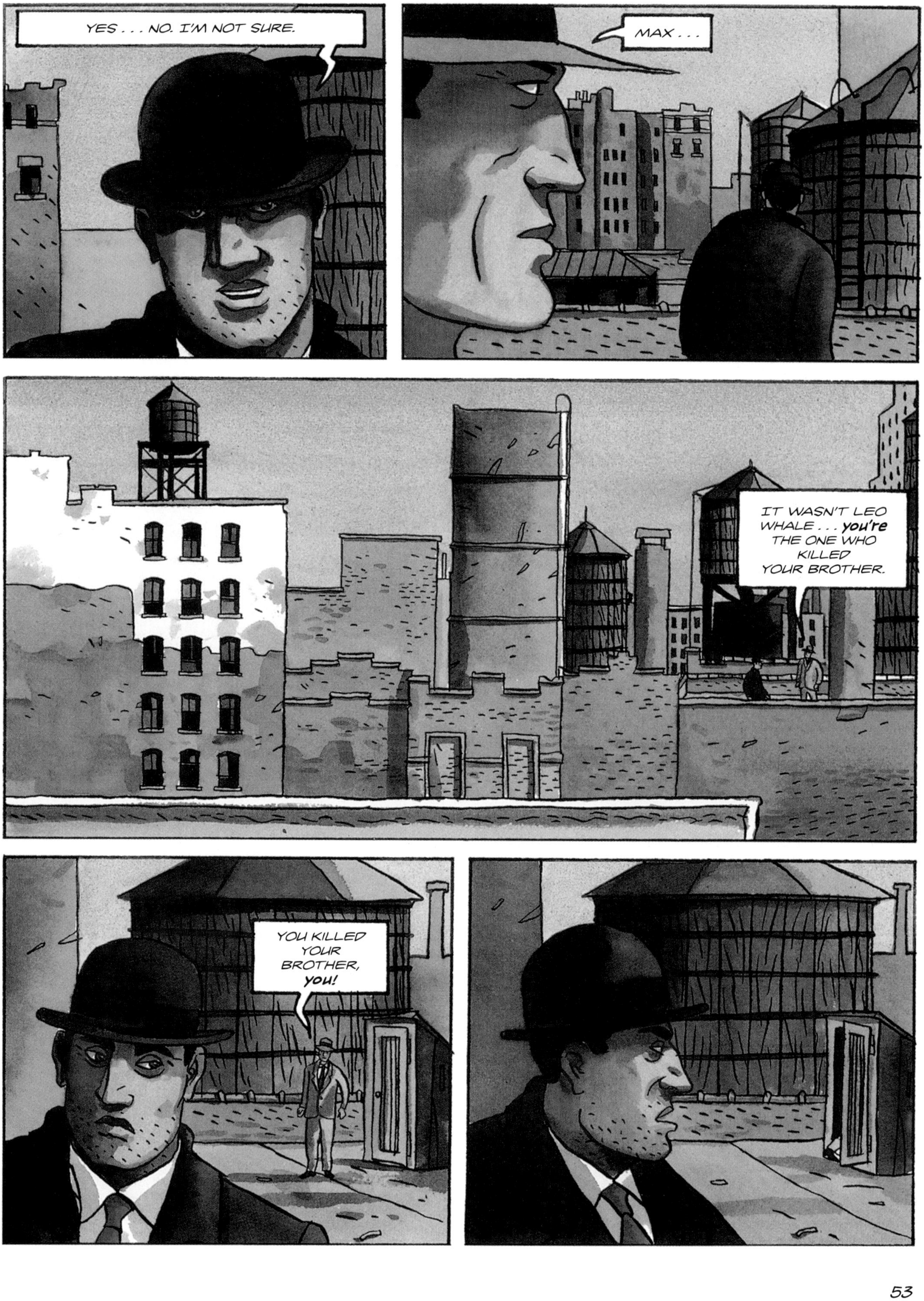
YES . . . NO. I'M NOT SURE.
MAX . . .
IT WASN'T LEO WHALE . . . you're THE ONE WHO KILLED YOUR BROTHER.
YOU KILLED YOUR BROTHER, you!

THE RIVER RATS VS. SHERIFF STREET. MAX ISN'T THERE. LIKE A GREAT LORD, HE WAITS AT MENDEL'S TO LEARN THE OUTCOME OF THE WAR. QUEENIE, HIS OWN RIGHT HAND, LEADS THE BOYS INTO BATTLE.

QUEENIE, MY DAPPER BOY, COME. I'M WAITING . . .

I'M HERE, LEO. IT WILL BE MY PLEASURE TO SET YOU STRAIGHT.

QUEENIE HAS A LOOK AS WILD AS LEO WHALE. A MUFFLED ROAR RISES FROM HIS THROAT.

A STORM RAGES, AS BLOW AFTER BLOW RAINS DOWN ON THE DOCKS.

SAMSON MCQUEEN AND LEO WHALE, STUCK TOGETHER IN A LAST DANCE.

HE'S LEFT US, OUR LEO.

THE WAR IS OVER. NO MORE MORRIS, NO MORE QUEENIE, NO MORE LEO WHALE.

THE SLEEPWALKERS HAVE TURNED INTO ZOMBIES. WE CAN SEE ONLY A SENSE OF ABSENCE ON THEIR FACES.

THE EMPEROR IN HIS CAGE.

THE EMPEROR IS OUT FOR A STROLL. HE'S WEARING HIS VERY BEST SUIT. BUT MORRIS AND QUEENIE CAN'T HELP HIM NOW, AND HIS EMPIRE HAS BEEN TORN TO SHREDS.

MAY I ENTER . . . PLEASE?

BENEATH THE YELLOW TULIPS ON THE WALL, MAX'S BOUQUET IS LIKE A BURNING BUSH.

I BROUGHT YOU . . . THESE.

MAX AND IDA, PRISONERS OF A STRANGE PENUMBRA.

IT DOESN'T PAY TO BE ALONE.

WHAT ARE YOU TRYING TO TELL ME?

ARE YOU FREEZING?

MAX BEGINS TO TREMBLE.

SAD EMPEROR.

NO, I'M NOT FREEZING. BUT PEOPLE COULD START TAKING ADVANTAGE OF YOU . . .

TAKING ADVANTAGE?

THEY COULD CLIMB THROUGH YOUR WINDOW AT NIGHT, OR STOP YOU IN THE STREET, OR SAY UNPLEASANT THINGS WHILE YOU'RE AT THE LOEW'S DELANCEY.

WHY WOULD THEY DO THAT?

BECAUSE YOU HAVE NO ONE TO PROTECT YOU.

BUT I HAVE SOMEONE-- YOU!

YEAH . . . I'M MORRIS'S BROTHER . . . AND . . . IDA, WOULD YOU MARRY ME? NOT RIGHT AWAY . . . BUT COULD YOU EVER IMAGINE THE IDEA . . . ? TO MARRY ME, I MEAN.

YES.

THE EMPEROR'S FIANCÉE.

THE EMPEROR MAX, LORD OF THE LOWER EAST SIDE.
ALL HIS VASSALS HAVE COME TO PAY HIM HOMAGE.

THE EMPEROR'S MARRIAGE. SHERIFF STREET IS
INTOXICATED. EVERYONE IS HAVING A GOOD TIME.

THE MARIONETTES OF SHERIFF STREET--WOODEN BOYS ABANDONED BY THEIR CREATOR.

AH, HERE'S THE HAPPIEST MAN IN THE WORLD.

MAX, CAN I HAVE THE HONOR OF DANCING WITH YOUR BRIDE?

A MANNEQUIN WHO COULD HAVE COME OUT OF A BRIDAL SHOP ON GRAND STREET.

SERGEANT STRONG . . .
MY WIFE, PLEASE.

IDA NAKED, LIKE A PRECIOUS JEWEL.

THE EMPEROR CAN'T FIND ANY WARMTH IN THE ARMS OF IDA CHANCE.

A LITTLE GOD LOST IN AN UNKNOWN SEA.

DO I GIVE YOU PLEASURE, MAX?

YES.

YOU AREN'T THINKING OF MORRIS . . . NOW, WHILE YOU'RE WITH ME?

NO.

IN ORDER TO WIN, MAX HAS LOST EVERYTHING. IDA IS A WIDOW, NOT THE BRIDE OF AN EMPEROR. MORRIS WILL ALWAYS REMAIN BETWEEN THEM. MAX AND IDA CHANCE, CHILDREN OF A PARADISE WITH YELLOW TULIPS ON THE WALLS.

Jacques de Loustal Sketches

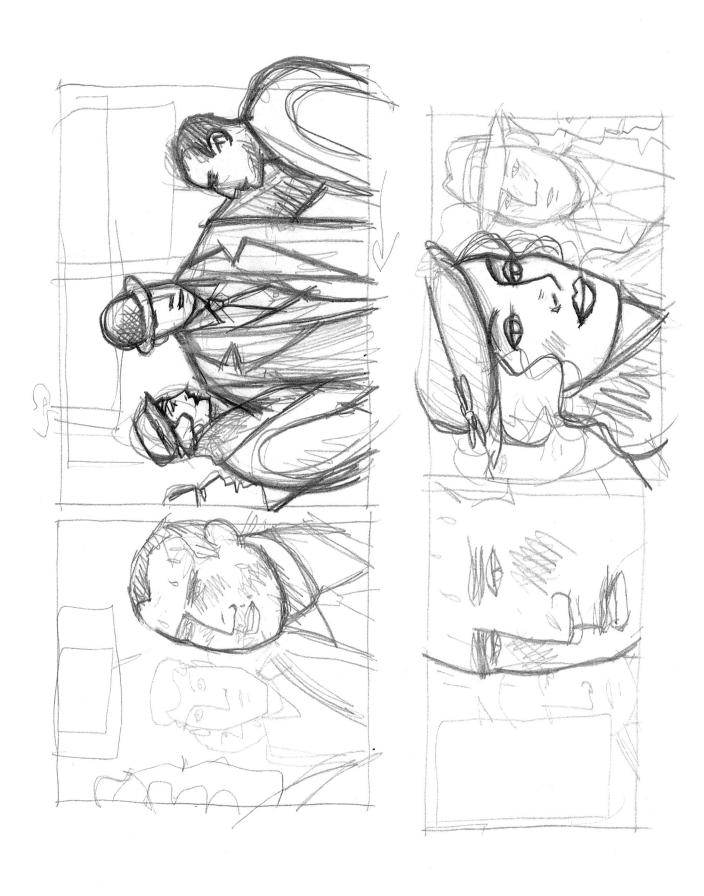

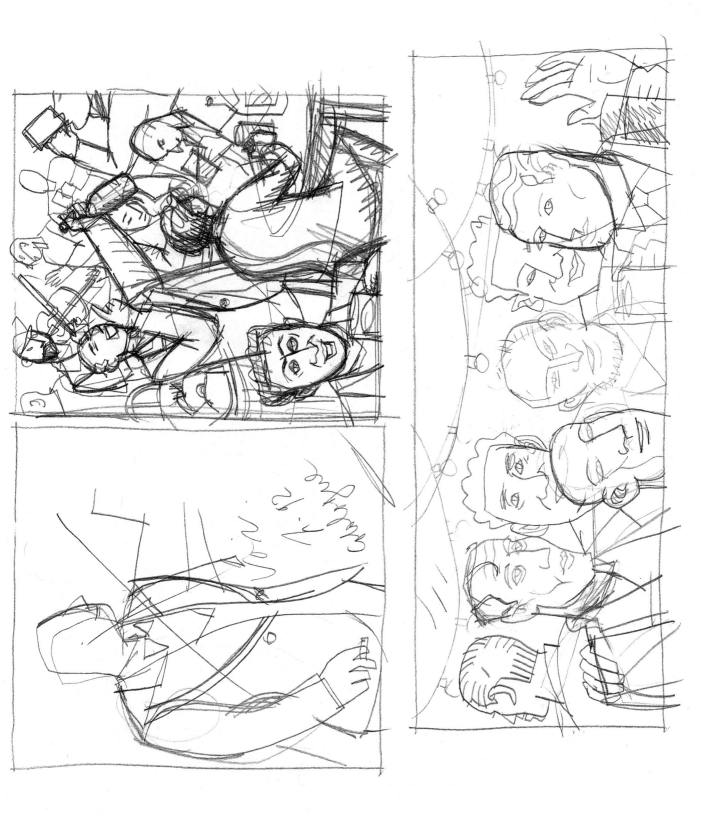

69

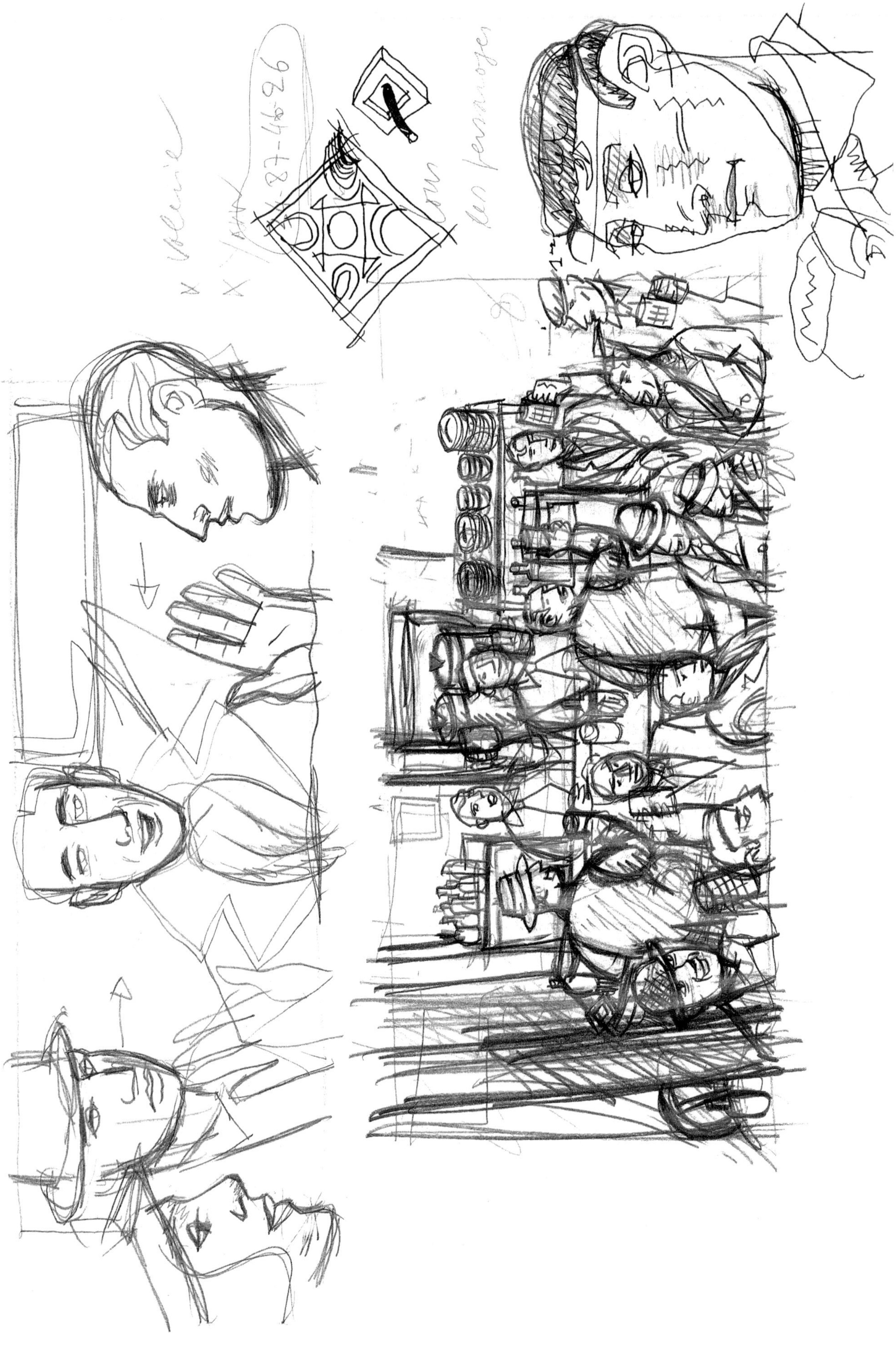

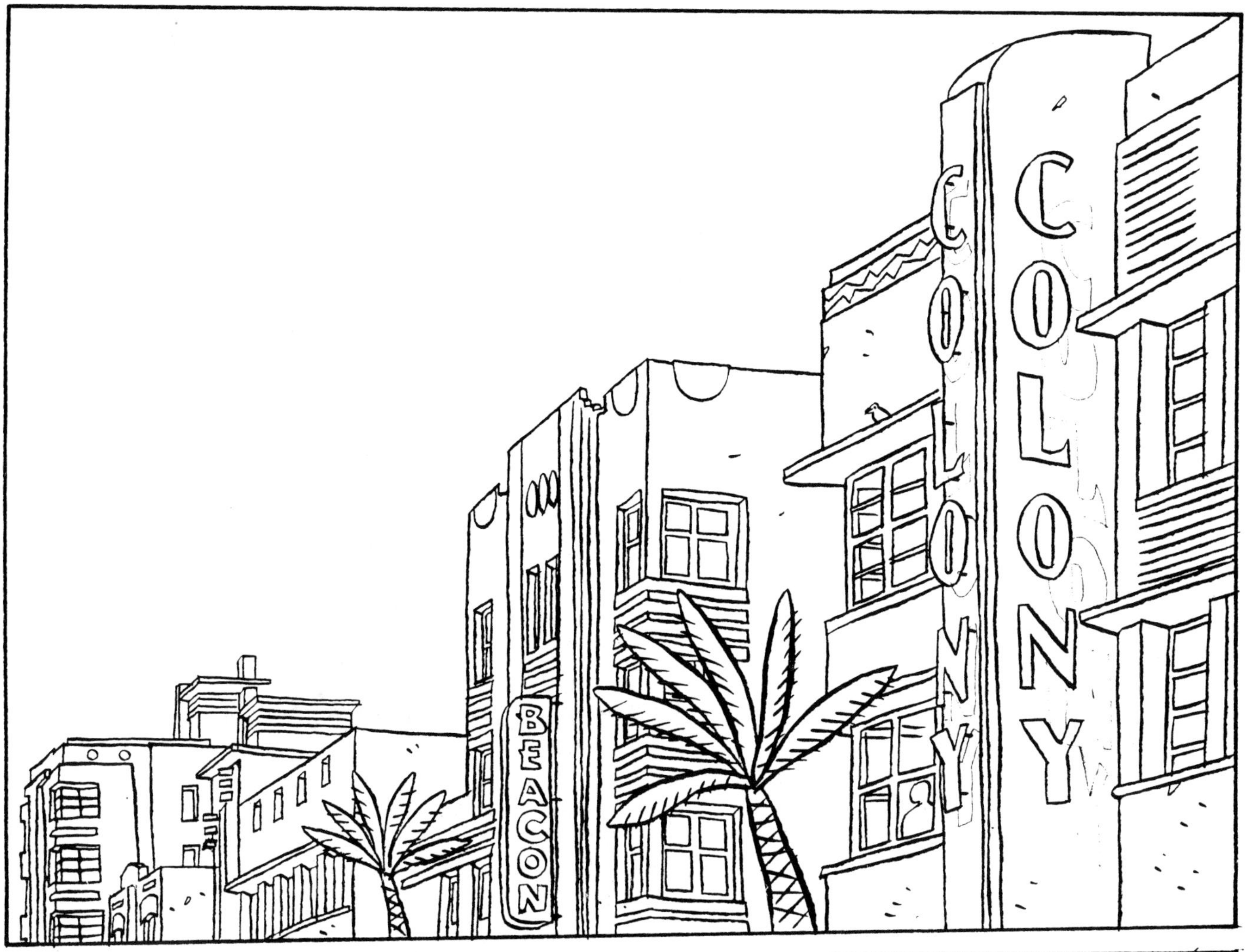
COLONY
COLONY
BEACON

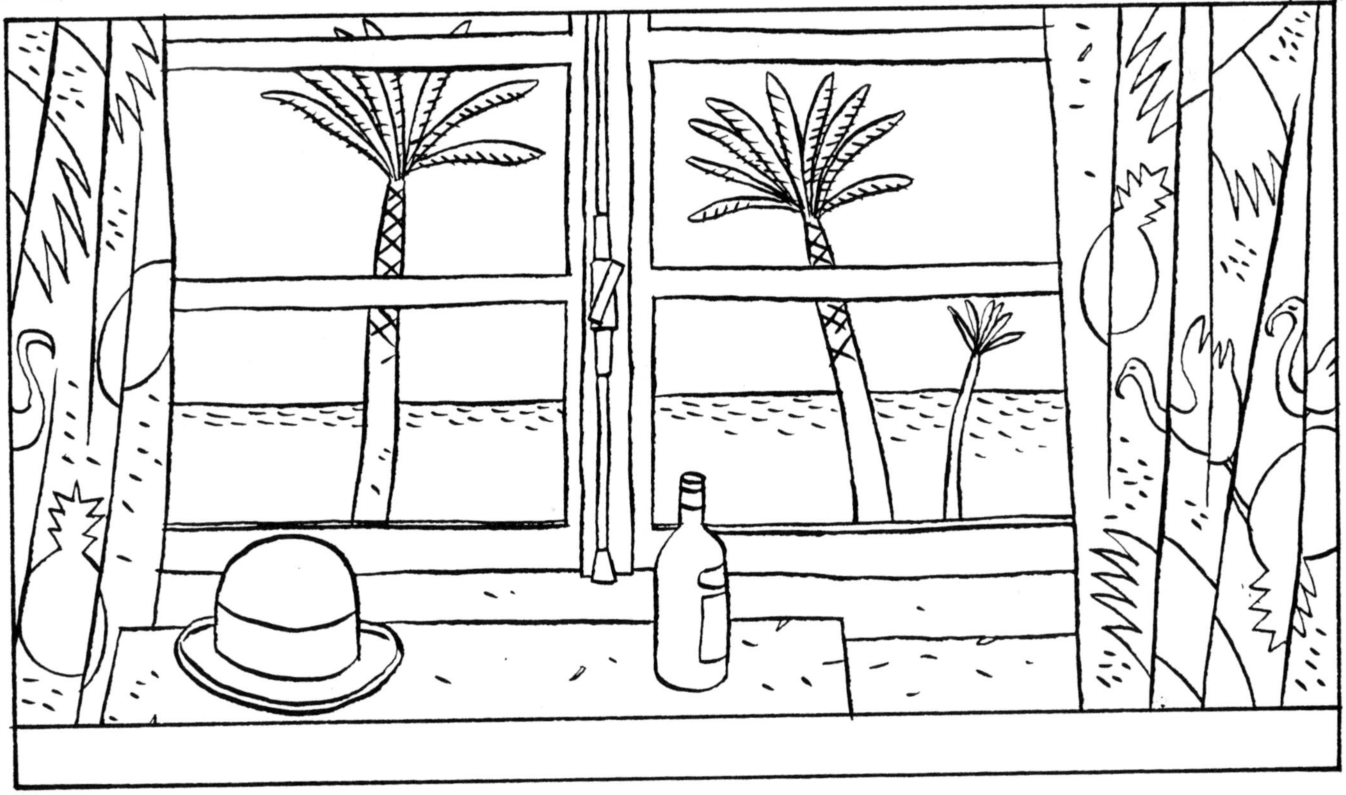

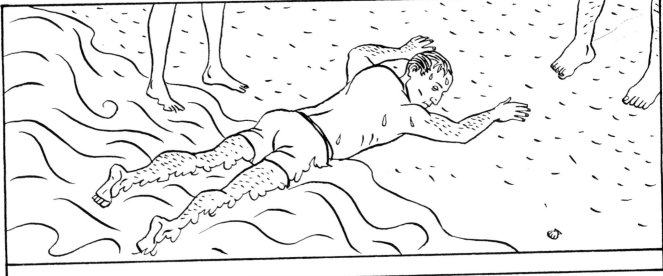
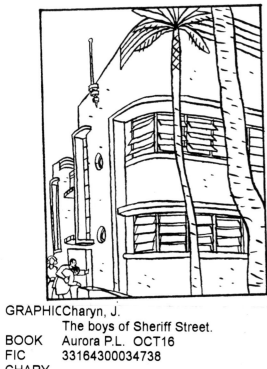
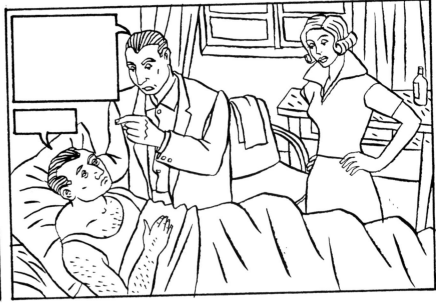